the unseen side of the moon

craig bristow

Matador
9 Priory Business Park,
Wistow Road, Kibworth Beauchamp,
Leicestershire. LE8 0RX
Tel: 0116 279 2299
Email: books@troubador.co.uk
Web: www.troubador.co.uk/matador
Twitter: @matadorbooks

ISBN 978 1789018 721

British Library Cataloguing in Publication Data.
A catalogue record for this book is available from the British Library.

Printed and bound in Great Britain by 4edge Limited
Typeset in 11pt Adobe Caslon Pro by Troubador Publishing Ltd, Leicester, UK

Matador is an imprint of Troubador Publishing Ltd

To my mother,
Sharon Elizabeth Bristow,
thank you for saving my life
and giving me
hope

Samaritans –
116 123
samaritans.org

National Suicide Prevention Lifeline –
1-800-273-8255

Campaign Against Living Miserably (CALM) –
0800 58 58 58
thecalmzone.net

Papyrus HOPElineUK –
0800 068 41 41
papyrus-uk.org

Childline –
0800 1111
childline.org.uk

Mind – Mindinfoline –
0300 123 3393
mind.org.uk

YoungMinds –
0808 802 5544
youngminds.org.uk

Bipolar UK –
bipolaruk.org.uk

Men's Health Forum –
menshealthforum.org.uk

No Panic –
0844 967 4848
nopanic.org.uk

OCD Action –
0845 390 6232
ocdaction.org.uk

SANE –
0300 304 7000
sane.org.uk/support
sane.org.uk/textcare
sane.org.uk/supportforum

The Recovery Letters –
therecoveryletters.com

The Mix –
0808 808 4994
themix.org.uk

Maytree –
020 7263 7070
maytree.org.uk

kooth.com

Alcoholics Anonymous –
0845 769 7555
alcoholics-anonymous.org.uk

Gamblers Anonymous –
gamblersanonymous.org.uk

Narcotics Anonymous –
0300 999 1212
ukna.org

BEAT (Eating disorders) –
0808 801 0677 (adults)
0808 801 0711 (for under-18s)
b-eat.co.uk

contents

warning

this book contains highly sensitive material. no poem has been selected for shock value nor written to be purposely morbid. nothing within this book is a fabrication, everything you will read is true and my own personal experience with mental health illnesses. scattered throughout are my musings on life and my opinions on today's discussions about mental health.

suicide, death, self-harm and alcoholism feature explicitly in these pages, as do two uses of profanities.

my intentions are to help other sufferers find the courage to speak out without apprehension, to overcome the unnecessary shame some members of society attach to those mentally ill, and to guide other people who may know someone who is suffering and can use the book as a means to help communicate with them.

talk. listen. reach out. stay in touch. seek help. realise your self-worth. be proud of who you are. you are not weak. you are not a burden. you are not alone. you *are* worth saving. the bad days will not last. do not give in and do not give up.

the mind

i was inborn with an illness inside
ingrained in the innards of my mind,
infested to feel incapable
which itself *i* feel inexcusable,
in life *i* am incapacitated
and innately introverted,
i am an intangibility
an inept invisibility,
this insidious intrusion
informs me *i* am inhuman
and was never an illusion.

– the i in bipolar

i am the sufferer of silence,
in silence the mind craves violence
where violence is struck like a tyrant,
a tyrant ruler becomes reliant
on oppression and confinement,
it is unruly not to be compliant
so i accept this requirement
and live my life exiled and silent.

the mind is vast and can become a prison,
creating an endless desolated sentence
to keep a person locked within for life.

there is a demon
who dwells under my bed
projecting hallucinations inside of my head,
an external struggle
of good versus bad
an internal struggle of not wanting to wake up mad,
blanketed underneath
prolonged paralysis
my eyes are wide to persevere passed callousness,
this nightly horror
in the abyss of my mind
has no concept or instrument for telling the time,
i outstretch hands in terror
to catch black holes of space
as treachery drops through and smacks into my face,
smothered by darkness
and powerless in-between
my dream is a nightmare but my nightmare is not a dream,
from a crevice of confusion
i jolt to consciousness
where the left behind slumber is now only ominous.
crawling out from cover
with sinisterness in mind
i learn *i* am the demon beneath who shall no longer hide.

the moment i realised
something was wrong with me
occurred at an age where all i wanted to do
was get grass stained knees
from playing too much football,
but it was at this age of innocence
i realised the mutterings i always heard
were not from the people all around me,
the voices talking over each other
were actually internal
like choir members desperately trying to prove
who the finest singer was.

— *verses of raucous voices*

i try not to converse
with the curious
voice
calling
callously
to me,
it's an adverse curse
always furious
where a wrong choice
results in fatally falling
down to mortality
with barbaric brutality.

– *dark words deep cuts*

how do you cope
with irrational fears
when your mind
makes them rational?

i don't want to let anyone
inside of my head
for even a few minutes
because i am barely surviving
and sustaining life in there myself.

i have pretended to be happy
for so long
i do not know
what happiness
means anymore.

when different situations
don't have the outcomes
i have meticulously planned for
or would be improbable to ever happen
in the first place
i still live my life as if they *have* occurred
exactly as i imagined.

i don't understand this illness
that comes from within,
because from the outside i am healthy
to the world looking in.
the illness may not be visible
but it doesn't hurt any less,
my life is overcome
with nothing but distress.
i can't explain
what's going on inside,
i am not sure i can face
what is making me hide.
inside is where i am safe
but it's where the damage has been done,
because on the inside is the disease
that has been here all along.

my body is accustomed
to what pain feels like
and its capabilities.
my mind
is forever open,
forever thinking
and forever evolving,
coming up with even more
excruciating means to punish me
in ways it did not before.

– *progression of painful persistence*

i have become
the thoughts
i am told
are un**true**.

repetition breeds normality,
my mind has enforced me to believe
the negative voice inside is right
and these feelings of torment
are now my entire life.

– *i am worthless*

being controlled by inner voices
confusing straightforward choices,
"you're useless."
"just quit."
"a worthless piece of shit."
each has its own voice
leaving me no choice.
echoing like an empty church
bellowing back with spiteful hurt.
on my knees with no intervention
or a prayer worthy of mention,
my body shudders and then trembles
as the next voice heard is the devil's.

– *childhood greetings of psychosis*

the past is regretful
which i want to correct,
the future is destructive
which i do not know
how to adjust.

– *kismet*

overthinking to an over-thinker:
you overthink the before, during and after
of one situation
then overthink the before, during and after
of the next circumstances
then overthink the before, during and after
of the next implications
then overthink the before, during and after
of the outcomes
from the implications
following the circumstances
which situated
after the first situation.

being stuck in these thoughts
never solves what might happen
but i am trapped in what might happen
because of all that has come before.

i live in phobia
of hallucinatory
consequences.

i am not sure what is more damaging:
words to me that have been harshly said
or making those words real
by repeating them over and over in my head.

i am surrounded by a family i love
who have been with me every step of the way
for everything i have ever done,
so why do i still feel lonely?

love teeters on the edge
of salvation
or damnation.

i am made up
from made-up thoughts
which have never been real
but have forged the person
i am today.

there is no middle
for i am either
bouncing off walls
like an incessant moth
unrelenting in flight
who ignores the occasional burn
for treasure aglow
or
i am hiding in the terrain
of a worn-down house
as a piece of second hand furniture
too usefully useless
drowned in neglect
and lazy whispers of
"i'll sort it tomorrow."

my mind has aged
like a forlorn wine
from a forgotten year
as it covered in dust
of being the discarded option
while the finer
and more appealing bottles
were chosen to compliment
the bragged about guests.

– in the corner of the cellar where light does not reach

the pain

how do i talk about
how i feel
when i myself
don't understand how i feel?

– "*what's been wrong?*"

anxiety is
allowing someone to drive your car
drunk
and blindfolded
on the wrong side of the road
while you give instructions
with your mouth taped shut.

addiction is craving vices
you know you shouldn't crave for
and cave to
yet it is impossible to deny
the want
and the need
when it is ingrained
in your life
more sensitive
than any of your senses.

i wish i could take pills of this
it's not that bad,
cheer up
and
it could be a lot worse,
i would have overdosed
on a cure of ignorance by now.

bipolar
has been cheapened
and lost its magnitude
after being depicted
as twist endings
forced into
poorly made
horror films.

– *"wait until you see the end! it was the same person!"*

these words trapped in my throat
hang around my neck like a
noose
i try to speak them but it tightens
i try to hide them but it suffocates
how do i ask for help
when revival comes
attached with a

¿
r
o
p
e

i stare at the bleak sun
and witness it get dragged down colourlessly
into the depths of the horizon,
blackness of night soaks through
like the flowing whiskey coursing my veins.
my knees tremble
but they are held in place by feet too heavy
and blistered to walk,
rocks crumble beneath my weighted stance
and splash down into the waves
vibrating this cliff i stand on.
i jump without hesitation;
i will find what i need on the seabed below,
this message will wash up on the shore
with the bottle i am sunk in.

– *destitute*

we force love
into all the small space we have left
then act surprised when it breaks.

these parties are all the same
usually starting by announcing my name
"where are you from?" "what do you do?"
just for me to ask the same questions too
i walk to the kitchen to find an only comfort
away from prying eyes causing me discomfort
i wonder what they think and what they say
i wonder how long is polite to stay
laughter erupts from the room i just left
maybe about my weight or how i am dressed
i take out my phone with nothing there to find
What's on your mind?
At this party i don't feel great
but it's hardly worthy of a status update
conversations around me and looks of obscurities
i drink more to try and hide my insecurities
here i stand as a person who is shy
and i begin to wonder why
this is viewed
the same as a person who is rude.

as i panic
my mind
casts out a net
and reels in
an array
of symptoms
all biting
and snapping
in the chaos
of trying to escape.

there is a thirst for my own destruction
which acts in a way of alluring seduction,
a desire where i always implode
a desire to comfort me when i am alone,
i need it more and i can't cope without
when empty i sow the seeds of doubt,
i push people away to stop them coming close,
even those who i love the most,
i do not want help from those who offer
my mind won't change so there's no need to bother,
i refuse accusations it is something i don't enjoy
this is my way to forget and also to destroy,
recovery i choose not to find
nor accepting this addiction has distorted my mind.

i always take *flight*
from situations
like a bird with a mangled wing
causing further damage to myself
as i *fight*
to fly away.

happiness is a stranger
an occasional
looked upon face
half-remembered
with feelings of familiarity
but a reality of unknowingness
so the greeting
entangled in my throat
is swallowed down
to be devoured
by what monstrosity
replaced the butterflies.
notes from a song
transport me back
to a cherished memory
yet i am unable
to pinpoint the time,
place,
song
or if the memory
truly exists
in the happiness
i thought it was.
so i purposely misremember
in case my brushes
with happiness
are not
how i recollect
and are all betrayals.

this isn't the first time.
another meaningless dispute
filled with words
we can't take back.
you walk out and i chase after you,
your words becoming speed bumps
which slow me down
as the   d i s t a n c e   between us grows.

soil rains down on the lid of my coffin
shovelled-dead-dirt hammering dogged and often,
i am buried alive
scratching at wood,
as my fingers decorate the inside
with rose-pricked-red of being misunderstood,
my nails snap off and i tear at the skin
blood drips from fingers to forehead down to my chin,
i suffocate from fear as i gasp for air
drenched in the sweat of this living nightmare,
the sickness in my throat is swallowed then consumed
to make space for breath in the crevice i am entombed,
with no idea of how long i will be alone
i look for small exits with the light shining from my phone...
the unread message is still on display,
i shiver and shake, this time unable to look away...
"where are you? everyone is here,
you can't have anything better to do instead?"
as i lay foetal on my bed,
come up with an excuse to stay at home instead.

– *here lays anxiety*

i exit the stage
to gasps from the crowd,
no encore tonight
as i am back again tomorrow
to play understudy in my own life.

– *all call for the beginnings of a doofer*

i do not recognise the person
reflected back to me in *the mirror*.
who am i
if it reflects the person i am disgusted by
who people keep telling me i am not?

– of erised

i look back
on memories of life
all framed in pictures of anxiety.

we haven't even arrived at the party yet
and i know we are going to fight,
i ask you not to drink
because you become a completely different person
and i drink because i want to be a completely different person.
i would have thought our problems
would be evident when we're sober,
when we have a clearer mind
of why we should not be together.
yet it is when we're drunk
we take it out on each other that we are incompatible
and we get away with spiteful words
because we wake up
and blame it on our lying liquored tongues
then kiss to try and wipe away leftover truths.

how often i get brushed away
into corners of speckled dust
forgotten about
until a decrepit sofa needs restoration.

i wonder how happy
we would be
if we could no longer share
how happy
we appear to be?...

– #happy #blessed #goals

here's an evil
and blood-curdling prospect
for an anxious person:
making plans.
why?
two reckonings:
the innumerable outcomes
of what *will* happen
coupled with the perennial horror
of leaving the house,
or
staying indoors
safely secluded
with the vengeful companionship
of overthinking
to remind you of how inadequate
and incapable you are.

i have hoarded a lifetime of masks for various reasons
none saved to commit crimes nor commit treasons.
all of this while i have learnt how to be guile
and paint each mask with a forced fake smile,
drawn in detail on each meticulously made face
to avoid any signs that behind there is a sadness to trace,
a disguise to hide my tell-all sombre eyes
a guise where nobody notices my deceits and lies.
i laugh to hide agony and immeasurable pain
to make myself feel apathy on what it is i contain.
every mask helps to cover what's beneath
to hide away the person who is underneath,
inquiries to how i have been you need not ask
when i have perfected these personas like a daily task.
all emotions painted after are still mine to fake
should there ever be a mistake where one mask does break.

– the comedy and the tragedy

we are still trying
to fit into a world
which has no compromise.

over a period of time
my back has benumbed
to the lacerations
from knives bludgeoned
into my back,
yet i am not blameless
because i constantly arm the culprits
with a tricksters knife
knowing my trust in them
the countless times previously
has resulted in my back
becoming a crimson coloured maze.
eventually,
space will cease
and the maze
will lead to my chest,
i know i will bare it
in desperate imbecility
because at least the next occasions
i can look into their eyes
and pass this off as the reassuring
friendly connections
i have longed for
while they recycle
the same blood-soaked blades
and i pretend the sharpness
will one day dull.

there is decay in my throat
i struggle to chew,
building up tension
and apprehension
where not just living
but talking
are tasks i struggle to devote
myself to.

– forbidden fruit of poisonous paranoia

if my pillow could talk
it would reveal words
i shouted in muted anger
and despair
which i did not dare
speak into existence.

a glass sits kiss stained
half-empty with your illusory words,
i drink it anyway to get drunk
so i can pretend its half-full
with everything
you made me believe yesterday.

there is something about ocd i can't explain
other than
there is something about ocd i can't explain
other than
there is somethng about ocd i cant explaiin
…
i'll start again…
there is something about ocd i can't explain

i can only be honest with you,
you see me through
on lonely night
to early morning light.
judgements eased
and the illnesses become freed.
"*don't.*" they say
but they will never know this way,
"*look how far you've come.*"
which is why i yearn to be numb.
from where i left, to where i lay
who i am, drank away.
a crooked neck and lubricated throat
as my gut begins to bloat,
i am the whiskey-sodden
and intoxicated downtrodden,
i grind my teeth to spark an alcoholic rotted flame
as there is warmth in this place of forgetting my name.

i bring my customary bottle
of being invisible,
the presence i have always brought.
clandestine conversations
as i accustom to the furniture as my monetary ally,
sinking myself back in want
of becoming pocket-escaping loose change.

– *"i didn't even realise you were here."*

your greatest trick of all
was to tell me
"*i love you.*"
while you disappeared back
to the person
who stopped you
believing in magic.

yesterday i was free,
allowed to be me,
the first time in a while
i found myself smile.
today it is back,
another attack
of feeling torment
and resent
accompanied by bouts
where i cry in shouts.
told not to speak nor weep
otherwise it shows i am weak.
left with more secrets to hide in places
and just hope i lose all tell-tale traces.

my life
is every coin
i dropped into a wishing well
that did not land
with the wish
facing up.

i see my reflection
and think i look averagely terrifying –
not good enough
to stand out in a crowd
but haunting enough
to avert plentiful pairs of eyes
to shut in shudder.

– *trapped in the mirror at 2.03am*

you sneak in from the night,
i pretend to be asleep
to avoid the truth
of where you have been
and you get ready
to lie next to me.

again with the tapping
again with the locking,
a made-up order that creates disorder
in my head,
where a bed unmade gets made,
where a bed made gets unmade.
t-shirts can't crease
so they get hung on hangers habitually
and increasingly
before i can cease
to give in to this thinking
rationally.
late for any event because time is non-existent
and i am persistent
with washing my hair more than thrice
until i feel suffice and alright
to leave and feel clean.
once, on occasion, i did a compulsion
incorrectly,
i came to a confusing conclusion
that the convulsion
caused from the earthquake
half the world away
was all because of me
and this unconnected mistake.
after obsessively
overcoming
my daily three lettered condition,

my daily three lettered condition
wakes me at dawn compulsively,
longing for a disorderly overcoming,
again with the tapping
again with the locking…

– 1, 2, 3, 1, 2, 3, 1, 2, 3

i shut my ears
to the ear-splitting 9 till 5,
alarm laughter throughout
filling the room with maniacal spite,
i wishfully wince eyes shut
to become curtains
while i lay in bed
and try to block
those gaps of light
which remind me a morning
is not always a new day.
life is just 8 hours a day
and 40 hours a week
off my life expectancy
where i make other people money
at the expense of my morality
and they tell me i am the lucky one.
each night is dreading the next morning
where the in-between
is filled with only dead-ends
i used to think were dreams
and what could have beens
while the awake has become the nightmares
i can no longer wake from.

the dens
i built as a child
were to hide
with the monsters.

– *please do not enter*

as i lay beaten
by those holding *sticks*
and others throwing *stones*,
i find solace in knowing
my bones will heal,
yet i know as years pass
the *words* said by my attackers
will tear open scars
to damage me beyond repair.

when i am depressed,
i drink,
i reach such highs
after every intake
of lustily longed for unit
that i mistake it for normal elatedness
and betterment.
when i drink,
i am depressed,
i reach such lows
for making the mistake
of trusting alcohol
and drinking myself
into the oblivion
of an unworkable anti-depressant.

– loop of the mistakable urge

my mistrust, your lies
becoming our demise,
messages read
while you slept in bed.
"*it won't happen again.*"
you lied, even then.
trust is hopeless
if you tell it less,
lies create mistrust
when you trust
to normalise
your lies.
i'm at fault too
because despite my love for you
when we slept in a different bed
brought mistrust into my head
that you were with another instead.
mistrust engraved on my face
became commonplace,
"i trust you."
but you knew,
i had lied too.

– *mis**trust***ing

after *I* reach the summit of a mountain

i throw myself

and the flag

which marked my

tr*I*umph

all the way back down to the bottom,

back to where

I

started because

I

know my best

w*I*ll

never be good enough.

— *I*

hearts are broken
as often as promises.
feelings are edited
as often as pictures.

we have given
endless power
to our thumbs.

– swipes of temptation and socially murderous words

a glass house stands
on a fractured foundation
stood for years and built
by an unknown creation
strangers rolled through
and threw frustrations
all visited from far and wide
and various locations
a few stayed long
and others did not enter
viewing the glass house
as a silent tormentor
the house spoke out
to all who would listen
"i am broken, i am smashed,
please ignore my condition,
all of these rocks thrown
have caused attrition."
advice was given to some inhabitants living within
"never heave rocks and please don't throw a single stone."
but nobody ever cared to ask
why there were people left inside all alone
who needed shelter
and did not seek destruction
nor play any part
in the house's deconstruction.

i cower the day
when other peoples
reassurances
stop alleviating me
and i begin to reassure myself
with the words,
thoughts
and outcomes
i had put into the jar
with the lid
which never quite
fully shut.

the wind whistles your name
across empty forgotten fields,
the ones i still frequent
from where we used to walk,
i pretend not to hear the syllables
as i purposely sit in the spot
where they breeze seductively into my ear.

i watch from my window
as people walk by,
cuddling the curtain as a slow song
plays in cowardice lullaby.
the lyricism; heinous
the nihilism; contagious.
in-between my ears go the fears
which careen my fears into tears.
the song specialises in repetition.
the song specialises in repetition.
wiped on a decorative fabric
of disparagement
i see the stained memories
patterned from embarrassment.
with one eye outside,
i enviously peer,
with one ear inside,
i simultaneously hear
a different song that starts to play
which causes me dismay
because it has never gone this way.
in perfect harmony, tuneless moving speakers
tune into the musical speakers.
now i hear for certain,
the callous melody
about the panicked person behind the curtain.

(homage to *Keaton Henson – Alright*)

i stand under grey clouds
as they spit out
every last drop
to make the sun feel like
it has never existed.
"*here, an umbrella for you,*" says the stranger.
"does it work?" i ask.
"*it might,*" the stranger says bluntly,
while handing out more umbrellas
to people in the storm with me.
after an initial struggle,
my umbrella reluctantly opens for me.
yet i stay soaked in the invasive rain
due to the holes above my head
which i am sure were not caused by weather.
i look around as those next to me
open their own umbrella…
umbrellas with the same pattern as mine,
with the same damage as the one i hold…
whether because of the damage or something else,
there are some who wave a tired hand
and reject the offer from the stranger,
instead choosing to look skywards
for a glimmer of hope
in the place where the sun
no longer exists.

after years of using stabilisers
i dare to ride a bicycle
unaided and on my own.
i surprise myself
with the distance i travel
all the while feeling
a fall is imminent.
i am shouted at by passers-by
to journey through
the oil of trepidation
and follow the lead
of those up ahead.
i witness other riders
cruise over hidden potholes
but i fall because of them
like a graceless eagle
swooping blindly
into what's between
a rock and a hard place.
bloodied knees,
swollen elbows
and deafening
cackles of laughter
tell me i should stop
yet i persevere...
now i understand...
i travel on with shame
because i realise the stabilisers

were never detached
from the outset
yet i *still* perished.
i endeavour onwards,
navigating through the discussions
about how far i keep falling.

it's hard to differentiate
day from night
when both have the same
long and lonely
stretched out hours.

i did not realise how painstaking it is to build a wall
i never consciously knew i was building.
pictures of intrusive thoughts hang on display
and though nobody will ever see them
i judge myself on the décor anyway,
the wall is left unpainted due to exhaustion
and because my eyes naturally recognise
the homeliness of dirtied surroundings.
on the other side of my wall
is where everyone stands and speaks at me:
"you need to let me in."
"how can i help if you don't talk to me?"
"it's your own fault for pushing people away."
the queue once formed has diminished over the years
as most people grew wearied of waiting
when their questions became accusations
and my answers were dumfounded and belligerent.
you see, i cemented this wall on the base of a lie;
it was *not* built to stop letting people in,
the wall was willingly built
to keep *who* i am
from ever getting out.

i am a child
walking lost and helpless,
my hands cling to knife-edged coat-tails
worn by faceless strangers,
my blood blemished fingers
drip ahead of my dependant steps
and i am too frightened to ask where we are going.
now unguided, my afflicted mind
leads me to an open tunnel;
enclosed in complete darkness i let out a whimper,
echoing cries bellow back in malevolence
as my eyes accustom to the surrounding
and claustrophobic emptiness.
i am trapped, confined in the tunnel i was once told
would have light at the end of its path.

depression

is ...

depression is…
crying, for no particular reason
but knowing that deep down inside of you
there is a reason why
and those tears want to escape
from the poisonous disease
eating you from within.

depression is…
the little voice in your mind
who questions *everything* about you
and your existence.

depression is…
being unable to swim
as you drown underwater
gasping for air
while people look down
and mime words to swim a little harder.

depression is…
not just listening to the agony
from your loved ones
it's empathising to the point
where you experience it at the same time

because your own agony
has taught you how to have
abundant emotional investment
in *everyone* you love.

depression is...
losing your voice
when you're out with friends.

depression is...
getting told to open up
but not being listened to.

depression is...
arriving at parties
where you isolate yourself to a corner all night
having conversations in your head
with every single person there
and every single conversation
leads back to them
belittling you on job choices
and not knowing enough about politics
and your face goes red like an open wound
before you've even gained the courage
to actually introduce yourself.

depression is…
creating infinite versions
of who you are
to prevent anyone
from being able to spot
the slightest sign
of how depressed you are.

depression is…
being given advice which states
"you need to get out and socialise
if you ever want to feel better."
"you need to learn
to enjoy yourself
and smile a bit more."
yet the same people who offer this advice
then tell you your depression cannot be serious
nor worthy enough
of feeling the way you do
if you manage to go out
and enjoy yourself,
smiling the way they told you to.

depression is…
turning your phone face down
from *anyone* attempting to call you

as the idea of unplanned interactions and plans
is like being thrown into an ocean of turmoil.

depression is…
drinking alcohol for the sole purpose
it works as an escapism
and for the duration of being detached
you can pretend that when you wake up
the following morning
you will turn over a new leaf of optimism
but the alcohol on your breath
keeps blowing the leaf away
and you are left confused
with how quick the seasons have changed.

depression is…
"a desired for fault
for those seeking attention."

depression is…
self-destructing.

depression is…
running out of reasons to use for cancelling plans

as you have clutched to the excuses
like optimistic lottery numbers
not realising there was never a prize.

depression is...
feeling you look the most presentable
you have appeared your whole life
and when people compliment you
you adversely remember the disdained looks that kill
which speak much louder than any pleasantries can.

depression is...
not "*being discussed more.*"
it's the three-minute-filler forced into tv talk shows
before the segment where you can win a new car
and a cash prize
or about how to save money on insurance
or the longer allotted time dedicated
on how to make a culinary dish you will never cook.

depression is...
like all mental illnesses;
tailored to the individual.
symptoms may be similar
but the experiences,

triggers,
sufferings,
thoughts,
outcomes,
reasons,
short and long-term consequences,
the stories,
the unshared anchored worries,
the length of treatment –
they are tailored to the
ones who suffer.

depression is…
an imaginary
grown-up friend
who dictates your life.

depression is…
answers to constantly changing questions
and questions to constantly changing answers.

depression is…
still defeating all forms of care
and medication.

depression is…
the timeframe of a few days
after a celebrity
has spoken out
about their mental health
and people use this
for their own personal gain
by pouring out affection
on social media
hoping for likes,
retweets
and shares
because it is more beneficial
to look like a caring individual this way
rather than for those around them
who do not have a platform
of being substantial enough
so aren't warranted
the smallest shred of care
or consideration.

depression is…
ongoing and advancing minute by minute.

depression is…
the worst day of your life
and living it over
and over
and over
and over again
and you can't get out of this trap
because your mind set the trap
and you blame yourself for falling in;
it's all of this, *all of this*, repeatedly,
every
day
of
your
life.

the reasons

having gained the knowledge
of my deepest and darkest secrets,
bipolar lurks behind me
like a vengeful ghost,
encapsulating my thoughts
and killing me from within.

– *a silent and invisible killer*

i am encased in glass
where time tips in circles
and i pocket sand
as a valuable commodity
to slow down the inevitable.
without knowing
where i am going
my life has spilt away,
golden sands of time
trickle through unknowingly
loose fingers
and gravitate
then evaporate,
minutes turn into years
and bring me closer
to the hands of demise,
i wonder if the passage of time
which has vanished ruthlessly
will waste away more hurriedly
now i have no turns left to rotate
or sand left to lust for
and i arrive on time
to a place
i once hoped
i would be late for.

there are unending prospects,
symptoms,
scenarios
and outcomes
to each individual strand
of my mental health illnesses
that i am unnerved
by the balance
now tipping heavily
to a dire end.

– survive_*die*

i puncture
and brand my skin
like a treasure map
where i follow
lines of blood
to spell out where i started
and where i might end.

– x

before i walk inside
i always leave my unspoken grief at the door
and brush it underneath the *welcome* mat.
i hide it away to deal with another day
although this is another lie i tell myself.
i hate going outside,
i hate getting social calls
because after they wipe their feet on the mat
i am left open to their observations
and insinuations of why i avoid public situations.
they treat it like a felony to say no to company.
there is another reason why i push people away
and prefer to hide from day to night and night to day;
the more i let them come back
and the more i go out just to come back,
the sooner the mat will fade
to reveal all i have tried to keep
hidden beneath...
my secrets
and *me*.

– fading home comforts

the road to hell
is easier to walk
when you are accustomed
to the burn.

– *reacquainting with purgatory*

i dig and search within
for a place i can find
to finally give up alcohol
but the deeper i go
i find uncountable puddles
which already stink
of my failed attempts from before.

in the gap where my heart is evaporating
is a black hole of space which is suffocating,
floating untethered in a place harsh and starless
i am dragged towards a void of darkness,
screams are futile, devoid of sound
i accepted long ago my body may not be found,
drifting away from all once bright
now enticed by a peculiar new light.

my head works like the rain
to ruin a wedding day,
it is like catching droplets from the sky to try
and draw pictures in my hand to understand
why it has fallen from so high
just to splash and die
yet still manage to reign over the day ahead
with dispiriting dread,
i pretend i am under shelter
to make myself feel better
and somehow snatch, catch and discover
why the day is draining of colour,
the downpour of incessant unpleasant thoughts
with which i have fought
and befallen to before
continue to shower in confusion and illusion
all around me
while the guests remain wide-eyed and smiley
as if the sun was still shining brightly,
but it's me who stands soaked and unhappy
in the moments i should feel happy.

....

painting palms with raindrops

there is no greater instrument
and vulnerability than the human mind.

– the fragile human being

how do i stop
the urge to die
if my heart
was already crossed?

– *needle*

i am loneliness
where even cosiness
is odious
in loneliness,
scared of being outdoor
i hide away indoor
where i can explore
and abhor
and adore
loneliness,
i know this is erroneous
and unjust
but i must
try to survive
because inside
my mind
is a mess
of loneliness,
i may look alive
on the outside
when i smile and hide,
but inside,
i am loneliness.

the whispers i hear drunk
are quiet
in comparison
to the threatening voices
which reverberate
like a megaphone
when i am sober.

it's one of those mornings again,
i went to bed hoping i would dream
of a life where i lived happy
but i woke up having never gone to sleep,
there's a hidden cruelty within a bed,
you can experience joyous emotions there
and long for it every day with fanatical anticipation
but when i lay in its arms at night
like a lover i have not seen for months
it now doesn't feel like it used to.
i lay abed fixated on how much effort
the second hand of the clock is putting in
just to move one second into the future
and one second away from the past
to make an hour of lost sleep feel like five minutes.
i arrive early with a heavy hand
to halt the alarming sound
before it screams into the dark
and i jolt up on a bitterly cold morning
while my lover stays in bed
and rolls back into the warmth of a sleep
where everything is put on hold.
i linger and fantasise about a sleep
where i would settle for the type of pity love
where routine outweighs attraction
as long as it means five minutes
of unconscious forgetfulness.

perhaps the gun will cure this sick
end evermore sorrow and do it quick
as i load the chamber and shut with a click
clasp back the hammer and brace for the kick
enclose my lips around the muzzle

pulling the trigger to solve an unsolvable puzzle.

– *six reasons for a game of roulette*

i have become fearful of myself
more than anything else,
my thoughts make fear a reality
and take control with regularity,
i do not like who i have become
and i am given the choice to succumb
to my desire of death
where my last breath
will be a welcome relief
from the grief
of a life i have wasted
as a person who barely existed.

– *an inhumane awakening*

i sit and hide in this corner of the room a lot,
the part where light can never reach
because why would the sun
want to waste its light
on creating a shadow
which was forcibly attached
to a lifeless vessel?
even the tears have lost all enthusiasm
in running away.
i never knew it was possible
to feel this numb without intoxication,
but...
i like it,
people say they like to feel alive
but i seem to thrive in dead forgotten places
where even the moon
hides its shine from me.

— *dead to the world*

i borrow days
and extend life
by inhaling
other people's words
of belief
that this won't last.
i choke
and choke
but cover
the suffocations
by strangling
my throat
to force out gasps
and exhale words
that it was
barely a cough.

as a child
i made a pact with death
and we promised
to call upon
each other
should the situation
ever require one of us
to help the other.
i spent my time
constantly reassuring death
that life will one day get better,
being alone means nothing,
insecurities will one day
cease to exist,
friends do care about you,
there is no meaning behind
crying yourself to sleep,
you are not to blame
for these thoughts.
as i aged
and as i tired
i forgot
why either of us
needed the other
to begin with
as the lines started to
b l u r
and i learnt

i had spoken lies
to my dearest friend
as the guilt took over
and i came to the realisation
we both wanted
the same ending
from the outset.

– i promise, when things get worse

i ponder upon
the facets of my face
and picture
a workable structure.
my left eye: life.
the bridge of my nose: control.
my right eye: rational thinking.
i have tried everything
to unite the three,
even wishfully shutting my eyes
hoping behind closed eyelids
the three of them will work it out.
with eyes sealed
i have never liked the way i look
so i cut off my nose to spite my face
and bring a bloody anarchy
to life,
control
and rational thinking
as my lips colour to an irrational reddening
to bring a long and lasting
madness to the sadness
engraved on my face.

i am asked
very often
"*how has your day been?*"
and my constant reply is
"not   too
bad   thank   you
               "

but those words
get thrown out of my mouth
from a piece
of shrivelled string
originally stating
"   a   good
     day   is   not
killing myself."
from the throw
to the sound
the words on the string
always jumble
and i have learnt
to craft out lies.

– filling in the gaps

for years
i have scourged between
convincing myself
and talking myself out of suicide.
when i talk myself out
i cover my ears
because even though the words make sense
i occasionally do not want them to
but a vice like grip around my temples
make the voices crush in misery
pleading with me to please end the suffering.

it wasn't until i had to miss
numerous social events
to realise who of my friends
did not care how i had been.
i would reach out
to see how they were doing
and if anything was wrong
could i do something to help,
yet the same level of interest back
would reach such low levels
it wasn't worthy
of a stone being kicked
not caring where it ended up.
weeks and months would pass
of the same interactions
and finally their interest in me
would peak in the build-up
to an event revolving around them
as i received the same generic text
sent to everyone
to check if i was attending
as attendee numbers,
pictures,
social media likes and loves
far outweighed the time-wasting
of caring to ask
how another person had been.
when i was unable to attend

they revelled in sending me
a personalised text
to remind me i had not been present
but never cared to ask why
as they used this to justify
why they had not taken
an interest beforehand
and now wouldn't need to after
because it was me who was
the selfish friend.

the severity of depression
is a person wanting to commit suicide
to escape a mind
they are tricked to think is inescapable…
yet we *still* refuse to accept this
as even just a *small* severity.

– "*it doesn't sound that bad.*"

i look at the world
through palm rubbed raw
unbeknownst eyes,
bloodshot from tears
so common in their escape
they depart like blinks
to bloom dead flowers
upon my watery weathered face,
i am reprehensible
for wasting the gift of sight
by yearning to be blind
due to my tortured horizon.

we are at a disturbing point with mental health due to people who preach with reprimand that mental health is a fabled bedtime story; one told to children by grandiosely educated adults who say people are naïve if they still believe any are real. sufferers then have to categorically deny trying to survive with an insufferable illness and will carve off their own tongue with a knife before ever speaking ill, because physical ailments are truth and visible while mental health is the lie and conveniently invisible. however, if a sufferer attempts to speak through their bloodied mouth and carmine coloured teeth, they are suddenly met by judgements, misconceptions, ignorance, blame and declarations of cowardice by the same abundance of superiors – which becomes perplexing because although these illnesses are myths, they still manage to know *everything* about them, and the cure to what never existed in the first place simply comes from the upper echelons bestowing their revered wisdom, educating the mentally ill on *why* they are mentally ill and addressing those "issues". so to avoid *talking, fucking talking*, a sufferer is left to wander a coerced path which clouds decisions and leads them to conclude that the only way to halt the anguish they are truly living in comes from committing suicide. what do the deceased then get for taking their own life? statements of selfishness by the same socially surpassing snobs for leaving loved ones behind, and also, stupidity... because why didn't these mental health sufferers "*comfortably*" and "*openly*" just speak about how they felt in the first place?...

on new mornings
every time i wake
my best days
become
my worst days
because i am reminded
i am alive
still breathing

– "*the realisation*

darkness in Light

i want to stop the pain in order to be free,
it does not matter this outcome will only suit me,
the future ahead looks only bleak,
living in the now makes me feel weak,
a solution to what is hurting so much
any grip to what is real i can no longer clutch,
the freedom i need is in a dark solution
the outcome ends with my own execution,
a loving touch won't stop what's ahead
i will shut my eyes and welcome being dead.

hope

Light in darkness

i am close to the end of a life
i do not want to lead,
i want to stop everything
in order to be freed.
i am ready to shut my eyes
and welcome the dark night,
this is now a life for which
i will no longer fight.
i hold the blackness of death
in the palms of my hands,
looking for a way back
is in faraway lands.
i clench pain as i journey
on the soles of wounded feet,
i falter and fall,
signifying my defeat.
overhead of where i lay
is the ominous dark grey sky,
clouds form and i wonder when i die
will people ever know why?
a surprise second of doubt
turns into a minute of reflection:
can i live with my infections
and have my life change direction?
suddenly the sun climbs
and i feel unforeseen warmth on my face…
the land ahead and all around
is now a much brighter place.

still breathing
i am alive
because i am reminded
my worst days
become
my best days
every time i wake
on new mornings.

of wanting to live."

if i had opened up to her
all of those years ago
my mother
would have given me the bravery
and strength
i was certain i never had.

– *broken*

once the words
and secrets get released
they stop impacting you,
influencing you
and moulding you.

– *talk*

we think about the past as if we can alter it,
to change what went wrong
and what we could have done differently,
we're impatient to know the future
and crave to know what comes next,
as that time unfolds we forget
we are *in* the present
with a freedom of choices
to stop the past holding us back
and a future we are yet to live.

– *embrace* freedom

hope gets drowned
when it is searched for
at the bottom of a bottle.

i was reduced to nothing,
my mother helped to build me back up
into much more than just something.

my mother sacrificed her world
to give us the world.

everything that has happened to me
has made me the person i am today,
i have learnt all i have because of my past,
it has taught me much about myself and life
which i would not have been afforded
had they not occurred.

– *the recovered wished upon coins*

you should never
have to convince someone
to love you.

imagine the number of people we could help
if we were able to *talk* freely
and *unashamedly*
about depression.

i leave myself out in the rain
like worn out neglected shoes,
laced in holes and coloured by mud,
corroded heels from places left behind
and history etched in frail soles…
i hope that one day
someone will find them for good use.

you can't change yesterday
you can fix today
you will live for tomorrow.

feeling lost
can take you exactly
where you want to be.

even the sun
rises up
from darkness
in the hope
of cheering
everyone's day.

only lies
have unnecessary
details.

what we have in life
can always be replaced.
who we have in life
is irreplaceable.

do not give up now
because everything
that could have already consumed you,
could have already ravaged you
and could have already beaten you,
has been defeated,
by *you*.

the only benefit
of holding death
in my hands
was to find out
what life truly means.

you are not defined by the job you occupy,
you are defined by the person you choose to be.
we wrongly measure success
and contentment
on job occupations and salaries
and judge others
from a checklist inked in snobbery.
you do not need to compare who you are,
what career you have decided upon
and what you have or do not have in life
to *anyone*,
the value you hold as a person
and continuing to become a better person
far outweighs any job or any purchase.

whatever path you walk,
any progress is good progress,
it does not matter how little it may be
it is still steps moving farther away from yesterday.
when you are ready,
you get to decide
which day
will be the first step
to the rest of your life.

i expected a change to come
or for someone to do it for me
and forgot it was *i*
who had the power
to make a change.

all hindsight creates is remorse
and self-loathing
because you look back at the past
fixating countless times
on all of the moments
you wish had gone differently
or you could now do differently,
but those moments
can never be changed
nor adjusted accordingly.
hindsight is
– pointlessly –
being obsessed
with somehow
fixing the before
only to punish yourself in the now.
the past has always been history to learn from.

not everyone
who comes into your life
is meant to stay forever,
nor should they,
some pass through
and you learn lessons
about life,
about yourself
and what you *are* capable of.

you changed me.
i lost you...
but found who i am.

i learnt more about you
from the way you left
than i ever did
in all of the years
we spent together.

the *only* aspects and features
that should set us apart
from each other
is our individuality.

– *ignorant and imbecilic isms and phobias*

i write
to take out
the portions
of my mind
i can stomach
and digest
when
i am ready to.

there is comfort in being spoken to by birds
who wake each morning
in a spirit of knowing
they can take flight and be free,
i love the moment of waking
and hearing them communicate
in such melodic sounds,
it makes me grateful to be alive
when i think of myself
having that same freedom
once i am ready to use
the wings i had clipped
when heights seemed impossible to soar.

i will know
i am in control
of my illnesses
when life
embraces me
like an old friend.

– *compos mentis*

you can't become brave
without originally being fearful,
you *become* brave by overriding fear.

– an unlikely companionship

your biggest conflicts
and fights,
all that you told yourself
you would never get over
and never forget...
you're here, getting over
and slowly forgetting.

you always find out who a person truly is
when you don't owe them anything.
you learn more about your friends
when you are learning the most about yourself.
it's when you feel like you don't have anyone
that you will learn who truly cherishes you
as much as you do them.

a commonality we all have is,
unfortunately, one day we will die.
what we do before that moment
and who we do it with
is what counts the most,
because time, once it's gone,
is irreversible.

an unfortunate lesson i came to master
was experiencing heartbreak and the untimely disaster.
what once was mine and mine was yours
we shared secrets to climb walls
and open up doors.
the walls i built to stop letting people in
i let you scale without even thinking.
the cracks you may have seen along the climb
i pretended to build over to show they weren't mine.
eventually you left and tore my walls down
you then locked your own doors as my tears made me drown.
my ideas of love all became shattered
because i was made to feel like i never even mattered.
my foundation i had built for all of those years
was destroyed and washed away by all of my tears.
the new castle you had built and those fortress of doors
did not include me because i was no longer yours.

life changes as do our dreams.
growing up has helped me to see
what dreams are authentic and achievable.
failing at what i thought i wanted to do
and how i wanted to live
made me become who i am.
my life became treasured because of those failings.
failure *is* an option
because it leads you to somewhere else,
to something else,
to someone else.
living with regret is a lot worse
than living through occasions of failure.

after trailing hopelessly on the hotbed of a desert
surrounded by coarseness
as far as the eyes can see,
you continue to crawl
and burn your palms on yellow peril.
if you hold on to anything
it has to be hope,
cusp it in your hands
like it's the first sign of water you've held
after a duration now hazy,
the help offered
from those standing out in the burn with you
are not mirages created within your mind,
they can be the lifeline
to support your fight for life
and help you to realise
that when the rain finally arrives
it doesn't always have to result in seclusion
and murkiness.

i am the
man
i am
because of the
wo*man*
who raised me.

– *s.e.b*

when we met, i knew
i couldn't imagine me without you,
our life together
spoken like we would be forever,
the love was real
as i finally got to feel
the emotion
and devotion.
then words got said,
a coldness in bed,
life up ahead
on my own instead.
you've moved on, found another
to call a lover,
but the love before wasn't a mistake
even though i learnt real heartache
and why a soul can break.
our life together now apart,
a broken heart
mends with time,
yours beating already, but i still wait on mine.

true love
transcends
distance and time.

time is the most vicious
but most precious oddity
we don't realise its impact.
we get older and are too quick
to wish time away
to get to moments and events
that we waste all of the time
in-between of getting to them.
this can lead us to wait
even longer for happiness
or ever having it arrive
because life before those wants are wasted
and all of the moments to the next are hurried.
time then feels much shorter
but it's as we get older
time can take on a new meaning
because we learn *who* is important to us;
they help us to slow down time,
they make the time in-between
any moment, event or want
cherished and not wasted.

i keep wearing this watch
and witness time bleed away,
but i know that over time,
it will heal these scars.

the smell of a new book
transports me to places
i can visit, journey and explore
within my imagination
where i can forget the reality
of what is happening within me.

– draco dormiens nunquam titillandus

don't react outside
of how you would normally feel
to quell a feeling
you never normally have.

if. we. took. obstacles. out. of. the. way. for. people.
suffering. with. mental. health. illnesses. this. would.
have. been. quicker. to. understand.

the people who have suffered the most,
the people who are the saddest
are normally the ones
who are the most compassionate,
caring, understanding
and charitable with their time.
they know and have experienced
what it's like to feel ill
and insignificant
and they don't want anyone they know
or anyone around them to ever feel like they have.

i loved you too much, if that was possible,
i loved you so much
that i actually gave you the entire person i was,
i had become who you wanted me to be.
i unknowingly changed
the entire person you said you fell in **love** with
to become a person i hoped you would stay in love with.
even in your hardship, in order to try and help you
i became us – dual roles of **my** old self
and a new **self** if it meant helping you.
in a last ditch attempt to save what we had
i gave you the clothes off my back
to leave myself naked
and exposed,
to **heal** you **through** any touch i could.
it was when i did this, it was in that moment you said
i was the one who had changed;
i no longer looked how you desired.
you had controlled me passed the point of completion
and decided to destroy a project you got bored with,
leaving me to fix myself
from the broken pieces you deemed worthless.
now with what's left of my old self
and a self with you,
i am left not truly **knowing who i** am,
who **am** i now if i don't
recognise myself from all i have left to hold?

– a certain romance, hidden between the lines
(homage to *Vivid Vega*)

love is never to blame
it's who you gave that love to,
people break what they choose
and justify actions by claiming
it was never love for them
to begin with.

those carefree nights
where no alarm
needs to be set
for the next morning.
the following morning
where you only
need to wake
to the homeliness
of alarm clock coffee.

give me evenings
with the shy,
the recluses,
the introverts,
the ones who
attentively
listen to your words,
the ones who show
their embarrassment
with red faces,
the ones who forego
all plans and feelings
if it means helping
just one person,
the weird ones,
the bullied ones,
the ones who were
made to feel
anything but special,
the quietly brave,
the anxious ones,
the confused,
the ones made
to feel insecure
about their appearance,
the lost,
the "are you sure
you're ok? can i

do anything at all
to help?" ones,
the overly cautious,
the worriers,
the avoiders
of parties
and clubs
and public places,
the empathetic ones,
the over-thinkers,
the criers,
the misunderstood ones,
the panicky ones,
the terrified ones,
the old romantics,
the hopeless romantics,
the awkward,
the socially inept,
the real ones,
the true ones;
the special ones.

i am looking forward to getting older,
i can't wait to see the wonder
and hopefulness i owe myself and my life,
to grab it all like the illnesses grabbed me
but to never let go of the optimism i can create.
the world doesn't owe me
nor do any of the people in it.
my happiness will come
by what i allow it to be
and what i want it to be.

suicide will not end the agony,
it ends the chance of living a life
you *deserve* to lead,
suicide ends the chance of realising
you *deserve* to be happy,
suicide ends the chance of a future
you get to pick.

there is no better time
than right now
to do everything
you have ever dreamed of in life

– *the beginning of your story*

a special thank you

Dr. Victoria Barber

Katrina Wilson-Smith

Siobhan Fernando

Dr. Imran Malik

Andy Bissell

References

Draco dormiens nunquam titillandus
The Mirror of Erised
from the *Harry Potter* book series by *J.K. Rowling*

Keaton Henson – Alright from the album *Kindly Now*

Vivid Vega author of the books *Words That Kill*
and *Our Wild Mind*